THE OZONE HOLE

© Aladdin Books Ltd 1992

*First published in
the United States in 1993 by*
Gloucester Press
95 Madison Avenue
New York, NY 10016

Design: David West
　　　　　Children's Book
　　　　　Design
Designer: Stephen Woosnam-
　　　　　Savage
Editor: Fiona Robertson
Researcher: Emma Krikler
Illustrator: Mike Saunders
Consultant: Jacky Karas,
　　　　　Friends of the Earth

Printed in Belgium

Library of Congress Cataloging-in-Publication Data

Walker, Jane (Jane Alison)
　　The ozone hole / Jane Walker.
　　　　p.　　cm. — (Man-made disasters)
　　Includes index.
　　Summary: Examines the function of ozone in the
atmosphere, the causes and impact of a depleted
ozone layer, and ways of dealing with this
problem.
　　ISBN 0-531-17405-0
　　1. Atmospheric ozone—Environmental aspects
—Juvenile literature. 2. Ozone layer depletion—
Juvenile literature. [1. Ozone layer. 2.
Man—Influence on nature.] I. Title. II. Series.
TD885.5.085W35　　　1993
363.73'87—dc20　　　92-37096　　CIP　　AC

Man-made Disasters

THE
OZONE HOLE

JANE WALKER

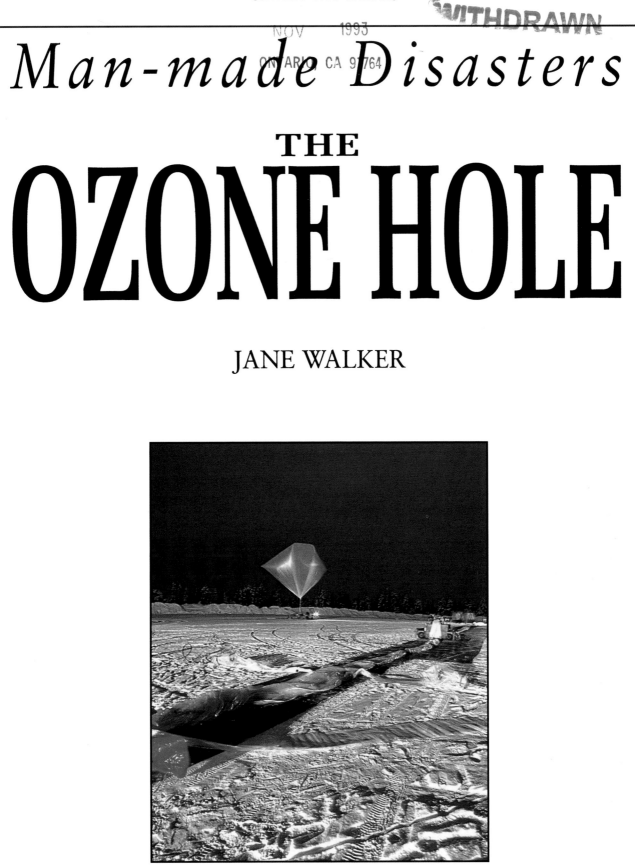

GLOUCESTER PRESS
New York · Chicago · London · Sydney

CONTENTS

INTRODUCTION

High up above the earth's surface, the fragile layer of ozone that is vital to life on Earth is being destroyed. We can neither see nor hear this destruction, yet it has been caused by human beings.

By releasing harmful chemicals into the atmosphere, we have caused this layer to become dangerously thin. An "ozone hole" has appeared over the Antarctic, and the ozone-destroying chemicals that are already in the atmosphere will continue to damage the ozone layer for many years to come.

The ozone disaster is, without doubt, a man-made one. Measures are being taken to stop the production and use of these dangerous chemicals. But are they sufficient to safeguard the future of the planet and its population?

WHAT IS THE OZONE HOLE?

The planet Earth is surrounded by layers of different gases. Together these gases make up the earth's atmosphere. Within the upper layers of the atmosphere, between 6 and 30 miles above the earth's surface, is a thin layer of a gas called ozone. This ozone layer acts as a kind of shield, protecting the earth from the sun's damaging rays.

In the spring of 1985, scientists from the British Antarctic Survey (BAS) were monitoring levels of ozone above the Antarctic. Measurements showed that ozone levels had dropped by between 40 and 50 percent. When half or more of the ozone in the upper atmosphere has been destroyed, scientists talk of a "hole" in the ozone layer.

By October 1987, this so-called ozone hole over the Antarctic was almost the same size as the entire United States. Its depth was as high as the world's tallest mountain, Mount Everest.

The hole

News of the ozone hole was first made public in May 1985, in a scientific journal called *Nature*. The hole has reappeared each spring season since 1985.

During the long, dark Antarctic winter, strong winds and extremely cold temperatures lead to the formation of thin clouds. Certain chemical reactions occur naturally on the surface of these clouds. When the sun reappears in the spring and temperatures rise, these reactions lead to ozone destruction.

▶ **The satellite maps (right) compare the size of the ozone hole on October 5 of each year from 1986 to 1989. The hole appears in blue, violet, and pink. Antarctica is shown outlined in black.**

The false-color map (far right) shows the ozone hole over the Antarctic (white area) on October 6, 1991.

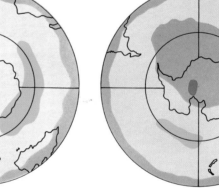

1986   1987

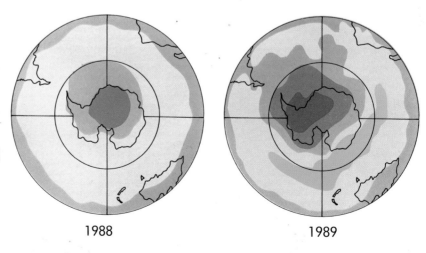

1988   1989

An Arctic hole?

Scientists measuring ozone levels above the Arctic region noted that ozone depletion there had reached about 17 percent of its normal level during the winter of 1988-89.

However, the temperatures in the Arctic are higher than those in the Antarctic, and the special conditions that help ozone destruction do not exist. At present, it seems unlikely that an Arctic ozone hole will appear.

▶ BAS scientists have been based at Halley Bay in Antarctica since 1957. They monitor ozone levels throughout the year.

In 1987, the BAS team was measuring ozone in the upper atmosphere using ground-based instruments. At the same time, American scientists monitored ozone levels from a flying laboratory (right) on board a converted DC-8 airplane.

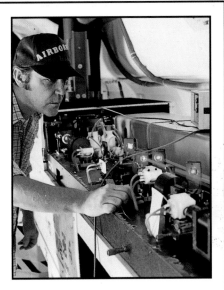

◄ **The 5,000 million-year old sun is a huge ball of hot burning gases. The sun is almost 93 million miles from earth. Although the temperature on the sun's surface is around 10,832° Fahrenheit, only a tiny amount of this heat reaches us on earth.**

Mesosphere

25

Stratosphere

5

Troposphere

Reflection
As the sun's rays travel toward the earth, more than 30 percent are reflected back into space.

Distance in miles

Troposphere
The troposphere is the lowest layer of the earth's atmosphere. Within this layer is the oxygen we need to stay alive.

8

Thermosphere

Absorption
Over two-thirds of the radiation from the sun is absorbed, or taken in, by the atmosphere, by clouds and by the earth's surface.

Solar radiation
Energy from the sun is called solar radiation. UV-B rays make up only a small part of this radiation.

Ozone layer
The ozone layer is thickest some 12-19 miles above the earth's surface.

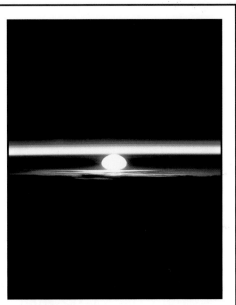

▲ **Without the energy from the sun, the earth would be a cold, dark place with no forms of life. This energy, called solar radiation, provides the heat and light that all living things on Earth need to survive.**

◄ **This diagram shows the different layers of the atmosphere. Beyond the thermosphere stretches the outer layer of the atmosphere, called the exosphere.**

THE OZONE LAYER

The earth's atmosphere can be divided into four distinct layers: the troposphere, the stratosphere, the mesosphere, and the thermosphere.

The troposphere reaches, on average, about 7 miles above the earth, although it is deeper at the North and South poles and not as deep over the equator. The boundary between the troposphere and the stratosphere is called the tropopause.

The stratosphere extends from the tropopause to a distance of about 30 miles above sea level. Within the stratosphere lies the ozone layer, which prevents the sun's invisible but harmful rays from reaching us on Earth. The dangerous rays found in sunlight are called ultraviolet radiation (UV for short).

The more damaging rays are the ultraviolet-B (UV-B) rays. Most UV-B rays are absorbed by the ozone layer before they reach the earth's surface.

A GAS CALLED OZONE

Ozone is a form of oxygen, the gas that makes up over 20 percent of the air we breathe. When the sun's rays strike the stratosphere, some of the oxygen within this layer is changed into ozone.

Ozone is a very unstable gas. It is continuously made and destroyed inside the earth's atmosphere by chemical reactions and the action of sunlight. This process maintains a natural balance in the ozone layer.

The layer of ozone in the stratosphere is beneficial to life on earth. But lower down in the troposphere, ozone gas is toxic, or poisonous. Ozone is formed in the troposphere when the nitrogen gas in sunlight mixes with hydrocarbons and nitrogen oxides. These substances are found in vehicle exhaust fumes and factory emissions. The result is a harmful pollutant called photochemical smog.

Ozone

Every gas is made up of tiny invisible particles called atoms. The atoms are grouped together to form molecules.

One molecule of oxygen gas (O_2) contains two atoms of oxygen. Inside the stratosphere, ultraviolet radiation separates these two atoms. A free oxygen atom then joins up with an existing oxygen molecule to form ozone (O_3).

However, ozone molecules can break apart very easily, and single oxygen atoms are released. They join up with other atoms and molecules to form either oxygen or ozone. Harmful man-made chemicals, such as chlorine and bromine, are present in the upper atmosphere. Their presence interferes with the natural balance that is maintained during this process of forming and breaking down ozone (see page 13).

Sunlight

Oxygen atom

Ozone molecule (O_3) breaks apart

Oxygen molecule (O_2)

► If human beings are exposed to the low-level ozone in the troposphere, their eyes, nose, and throat can become irritated and their lungs damaged.

The problem of low-level ozone is most serious in cities that are surrounded by mountains, such as Athens (shown right), and in those where there are large numbers of cars and a hot climate, such as Los Angeles.

Ozone as a greenhouse gas

Ozone is one of the "greenhouse gases" which keep the earth warm. These gases allow the sun's rays to reach the earth, and then trap this heat energy, preventing it from escaping into space. The way in which these gases trap some of the sun's outgoing radiation, and reflect it back onto the earth's surface, is known as the "greenhouse effect."

Ozone accounts for 12 percent of the total amount of greenhouse gases (see right). An increase in the amount of greenhouse gases in the atmosphere may have caused the earth to warm up by about 1.8° Fahrenheit in the past 100 years.

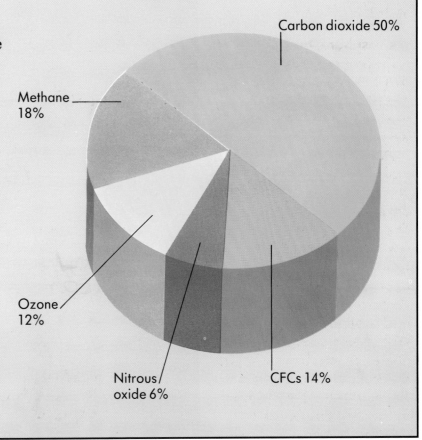

Carbon dioxide 50%

Methane 18%

Ozone 12%

Nitrous oxide 6%

CFCs 14%

THE OZONE DISASTER

Ozone levels vary at different times of the year, according to the amount and strength of the sun's rays reaching the earth. Scientists have now confirmed that a 40 to 50 percent ozone loss occurs over the Antarctic during each spring season (September to early December).

The chief creators of this ozone loss are man-made chemicals, in particular chlorofluorocarbons (CFCs for short) and halons. Once they are released into the atmosphere, CFCs rise up slowly into the stratosphere.

Here, they give off atoms of a chemical called chlorine. The chlorine attacks and breaks down the ozone layer. Halons contain a chemical called bromine, which attacks ozone in a similar way to chlorine.

Ozone loss may also result from non-CFC chemicals that contain chlorine, such as the cleaning fluid carbon tetrachloride. Another cause is the addition of huge quantities of ash and dust to the atmosphere following a major volcanic eruption.

► The sun itself adds to ozone loss. Dark patches, called sunspots, form on the surface of the sun. The appearance of these sunspots and other forms of solar activity (the yellow patches in the photo shown right) follows an 11-year cycle. Scientists believe that ozone levels are at their lowest every 11 years when the sun is most active.

One of the largest solar flares ever recorded over the sun's surface measured 365,000 miles. A sunspot photographed in 1982 from Arizona had a diameter of 50,000 miles. The sun gives off increased UV radiation during these periods.

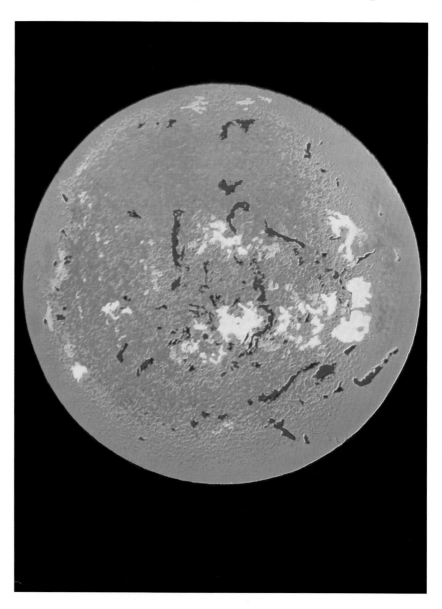

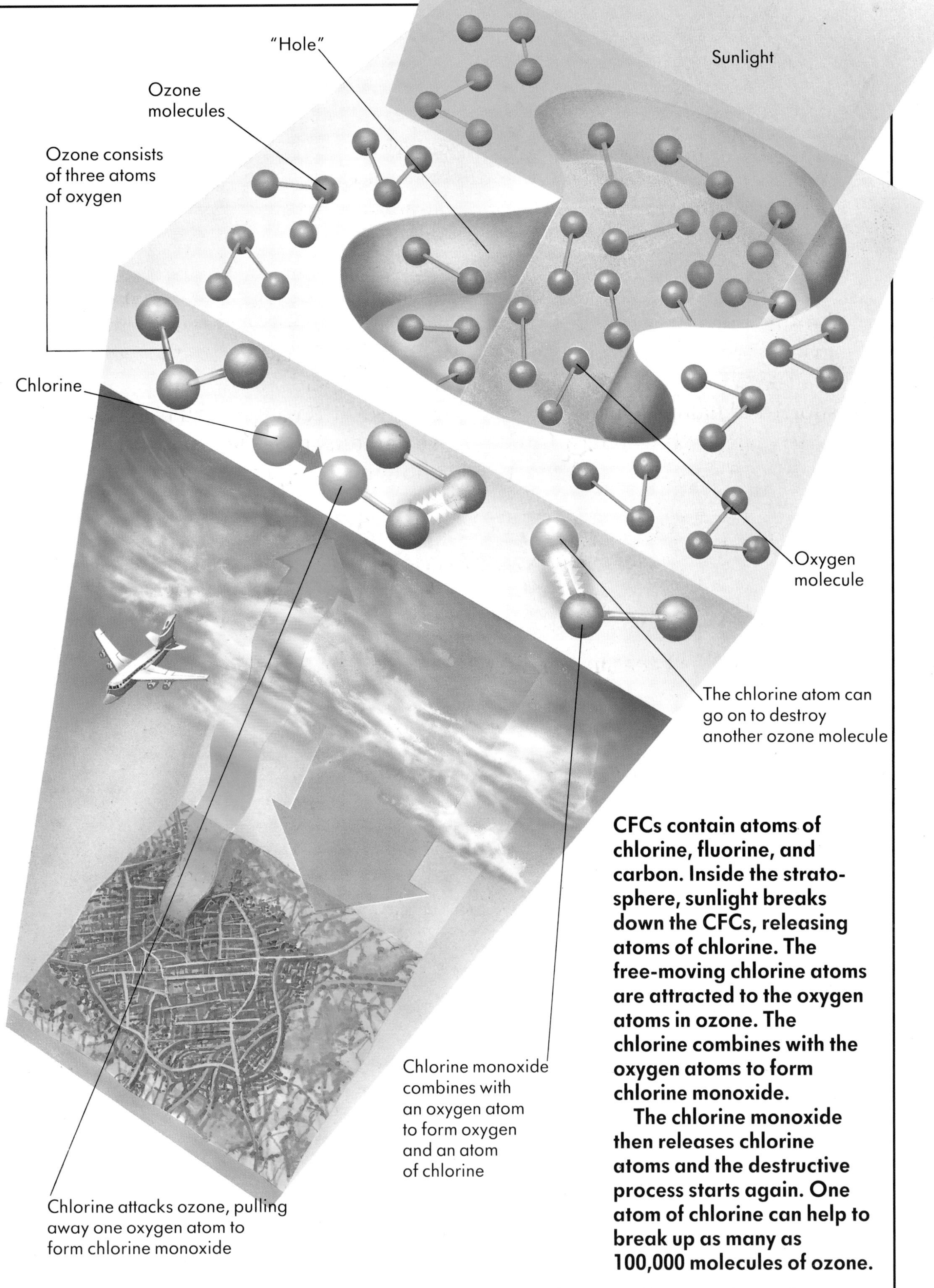

"Hole"

Ozone
molecules

Ozone consists
of three atoms
of oxygen

Chlorine

Sunlight

Oxygen
molecule

The chlorine atom can
go on to destroy
another ozone molecule

Chlorine monoxide
combines with
an oxygen atom
to form oxygen
and an atom
of chlorine

Chlorine attacks ozone, pulling
away one oxygen atom to
form chlorine monoxide

CFCs contain atoms of chlorine, fluorine, and carbon. Inside the stratosphere, sunlight breaks down the CFCs, releasing atoms of chlorine. The free-moving chlorine atoms are attracted to the oxygen atoms in ozone. The chlorine combines with the oxygen atoms to form chlorine monoxide.

The chlorine monoxide then releases chlorine atoms and the destructive process starts again. One atom of chlorine can help to break up as many as 100,000 molecules of ozone.

13

USING CFCS

In 1974, two scientists at a university in Irvine, California, Sherwood Rowland and Mario Molina, warned of the dangers of chlorofluorocarbons (CFCs), and their potential in damaging the ozone layer, causing it to become thinner. CFCs have now been identified as the single greatest threat to the earth's fragile ozone layer.

The principal uses of CFCs are: as a cooling agent in refrigerators, freezers, and air-conditioning units; to propel, or spray out, the liquid contained in aerosol spray cans; to manufacture, by a "blowing" process, certain kinds of plastic foam for packaging, for stuffing furniture, and for insulation.

CFCs are very stable chemicals, which means that they do not easily disappear or change into other substances. One of the most common and most destructive CFCs – CFC-12 – remains unchanged in the atmosphere for over 130 years, and is responsible for around 45 percent of global ozone loss.

CFC production

CFCs were first discovered in 1928. They are cheap to produce, they do not smell or burn, and they are easy to store. Their dangers were only revealed later.

Industry has already added as many as 20 million tons of CFCs into the earth's atmosphere, where they will remain until well into the 21st century.

CFCs are used as cleaning materials and solvents (liquids that dissolve or weaken other substances) in certain industrial processes, such as soldering and cleaning metals. In the electronics industry, CFCs clean microchips and other computer parts because they do not damage the plastic parts of the computer.

The pie charts shown right illustrate the different uses of two of the main CFCs – CFC-11 and CFC-12.

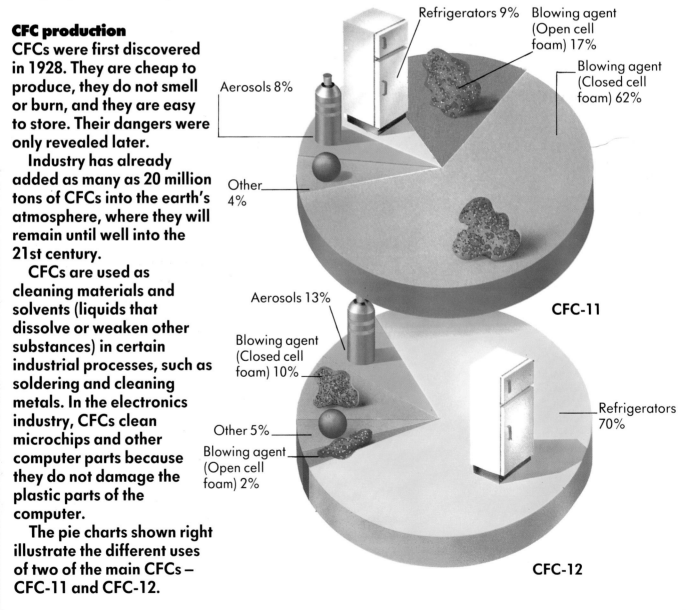

Refrigerators 9% Blowing agent (Open cell foam) 17%
Blowing agent (Closed cell foam) 62%
Aerosols 8%
Other 4%
CFC-11

Aerosols 13%
Blowing agent (Closed cell foam) 10%
Other 5%
Blowing agent (Open cell foam) 2%
Refrigerators 70%
CFC-12

► The graph (right) shows how the worldwide use of CFC-11 and CFC-12 increased from 1940 onward, reaching a peak in the early 1970s. Although the production of these two main CFCs is now falling, the amount of chlorine being added to the atmosphere each year is still rising.

A number of other chemicals have an ozone-damaging effect similar to that of CFCs. These include carbon tetrachloride, which is found in dry-cleaning fluid, animal feedstuffs, and pesticides; methyl chloroform, used in typewriter correction fluid and some adhesives; and methyl bromide, which is used as a pesticide for agricultural produce.

▼ CFC-12 is sealed inside refrigerators and freezers. If these appliances are dumped, this can lead to CFCs leaking into the atmosphere.

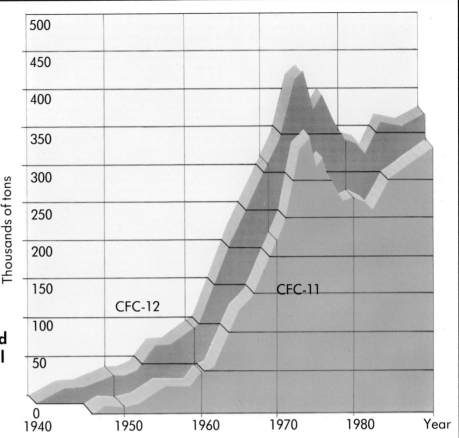

Thousands of tons

CFC-12

CFC-11

1940   1950   1960   1970   1980   Year

▲ CFCs are also used in car air conditioners. In the United States alone, 82 million cars are fitted with CFC-containing air conditioners.

THE DANGER

The ozone layer filters out much of the sun's ultraviolet rays as they travel through space toward earth. Only about 30 percent of UV-B rays reach the earth's surface at the equator, with around 10 percent reaching the tropics and areas further away from the equator.

As the ozone layer becomes thinner and thinner, increasing amounts of these UV rays are penetrating through to the earth's surface. UV radiation is so powerful that it can cause serious damage to human beings, animals, and plants. Exposure to UV-B rays can result in eye cataracts, which may cause blindness; in severe sunburn, and in the development of various skin cancers. Research has shown that even a one percent reduction in ozone levels could result in an extra 50,000 new cataract cases each year.

UV-B rays may also affect the ability of the human body to fight off some infectious diseases, such as bilharzia and leprosy, that enter the body through the skin.

Food chain

Microscopic plants, called phytoplankton, live near the surface of the sea. Tiny one-celled animals, called zooplankton, feed on the phytoplankton to form the first link in the world's marine food chain.

Within this chain, plankton are eaten directly by fish and other sea creatures such as squid. They are also eaten indirectly by larger fish and sea mammals, such as seals, which feed on the smaller plankton-eating fish. Even humans depend on plankton as the food supply of the fish they catch and eat.

UV-B rays can penetrate water to a depth of around 60 feet, killing the plankton in the upper layers. An increase in the UV-radiation reaching the oceans and seas could lead to serious shortages in both the marine food chain and human food supplies.

Zooplankton
Some kinds of zooplankton feed on phytoplankton. One kind, called krill, is the main food source of giant baleen whales.

Phytoplankton
Phytoplankton are at the beginning of the marine food chain. They absorb large amounts of the carbon dioxide we produce.

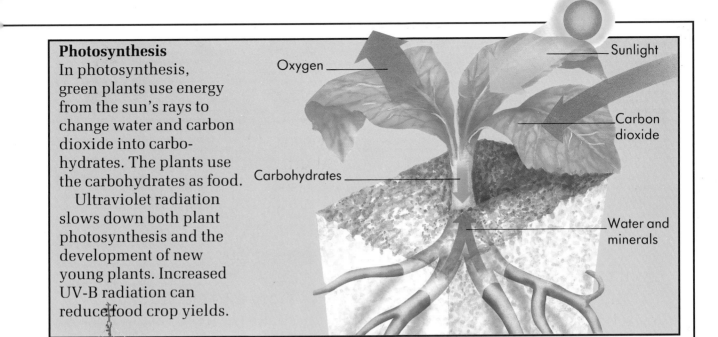

Photosynthesis

In photosynthesis, green plants use energy from the sun's rays to change water and carbon dioxide into carbohydrates. The plants use the carbohydrates as food.

Ultraviolet radiation slows down both plant photosynthesis and the development of new young plants. Increased UV-B radiation can reduce food crop yields.

Oxygen

Sunlight

Carbon dioxide

Carbohydrates

Water and minerals

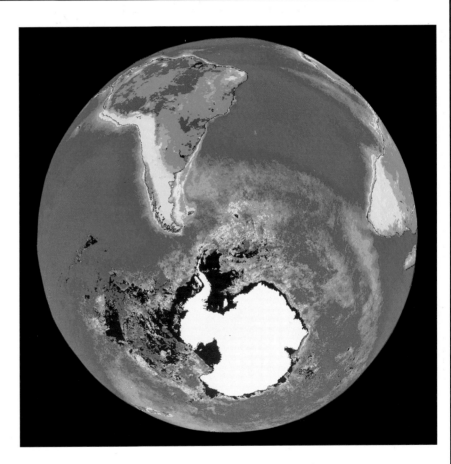

Humans
Humans are at the top of the food chain, removing around 90 million tons of fish from the sea each year.

Fish
Fish eat the plankton and are then eaten by larger fish and other sea creatures, or caught for human consumption.

▲ In the color-coded satellite picture of the earth above, the red areas show where the greatest numbers of phytoplankton live. The yellow, blue, and purple areas represent less dense populations of phytoplankton living in the oceans.

DISASTER REPORTS

The 1987 Airborne Antarctic Ozone Experiment involved a series of flights across Antarctica to monitor ozone levels. The planes for this experiment were based in the world's most southerly city – Punta Arenas in Chile. In an area between 9 and 11 miles above the earth's surface, ozone levels were depleted by an incredible 97 percent.

More cases of skin and eye disorders among the human population, and of disease and deformity in animals, have been noted in the area than in previous years.

The ozone layer over Europe was reduced by around 8 percent between 1981 and 1991. Even if no more CFCs are added to the atmosphere, scientists predict that ozone levels will drop even further by the year 2000.

In September 1992, the deepest-ever ozone hole was recorded over the Antarctic. Scientists at the BAS Faraday and Halley research stations claimed that ozone loss had reached a staggering 60 percent.

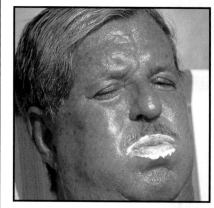

Low-level ozone pollution causes an estimated $4.5 billion damage to US crops each year.

Skin cancer rates in Scotland doubled between 1981 and 1991. Increase largely blamed on short periods of intense exposure to the sun.

April 1991
Environmental Protection Agency announces that ozone depletion over USA has measured between 4 and 5 percent since 1978.

Ozone levels in early spring over much of Europe decreased by 8 percent between 1981 and 1991 (double the expected rate).

March 1982
El Chichón volcano in Mexico erupts, sending around 500 million tons of volcanic chemicals into the stratosphere.

▲ The Environmental Protection Agency (EPA) has suggested that increased exposure to UV-B rays may cause 200,000 skin cancer deaths in the United States in the next 50 years.

When the 1987 Antarctic ozone hole spread across to southern Australia, New Zealand, and Tasmania, ozone levels over the city of Melbourne were reported to be 12 percent lower than usual. Skin cancers caused by exposure to UV-B rays are more common in Australia than in any other country in the world.

August 1991
Mount Hudson erupts in southern Chile. Volcanic ash and dust particles rise up thousands of feet into the atmosphere.

October 1992
Tip of ozone hole passes over Falkland Islands and Tierra del Fuego at the bottom of South America.

Pilot studies are under way to determine the effects of increased UV-B radiation on BAS Antarctic field staff and on land plants.

▲ **Exposure to increased UV-B radiation can reduce the yield of crops such as soya beans, wheat, rice, and peas. UV-B radiation can also destroy the nutritional value of these foods.**

January 1992
Record-high levels of chlorine monoxide are found over parts of the northern hemisphere. Scientists believe that the Arctic region is "primed for ozone destruction."

Australia has the world's highest incidence of skin cancer caused by exposure to UV-B rays.

A natural disaster

In June 1991, Mount Pinatubo in the Philippines erupted (below). Volcanoes add large amounts of ozone-eating chlorine to the atmosphere. Volcanic ash and dust also contain sulfur, which destroys ozone as well as absorbing the nitrogen gas that helps to prevent ozone destruction.

However, unlike CFCs, the volcanic dust and ash pose only a short-term threat to the ozone layer.

THE HUMAN COST

A decrease in ozone levels of just one percent could increase the amount of UV-B radiation reaching the earth by three percent. This, in turn, could lead to between 10,000 and 15,000 new cases of skin cancer each year, including a rare but often fatal type known as melanoma. This is just one of the frightening statistics about the dangers to human life from the ozone hole, and the increased UV-B radiation reaching the human population. Other statistics point to increased eye disorders like cataracts.

Skin cancers particularly affect fair-skinned, red-haired people who lack a chemical called melanin, which occurs naturally in the human body. Melanin causes skin to become suntanned when exposed to sunlight, and helps to filter out the harmful UV-B rays that cause sunburn.

Australia has the world's highest incidence of skin cancer. Two out of every three white Australians need treatment for skin cancer by the age of 75. In Britain, 7 percent more skin cancer cases are reported each year.

▶ Doctors claim that children are particularly at risk if exposed to high doses of UV-B radiation during childhood. It is thought that between four and five periods of prolonged exposure to UV-B rays before the age of 16 years can increase the chances of developing skin cancer as an adult.

▼ The malignant melanoma shown below is a highly dangerous form of skin cancer. Around 4 out of every 10 patients with this disease die within 5 years.

The occurrence of melanoma has been linked to people exposing their skin to short periods of very strong sunlight during sunbathing.

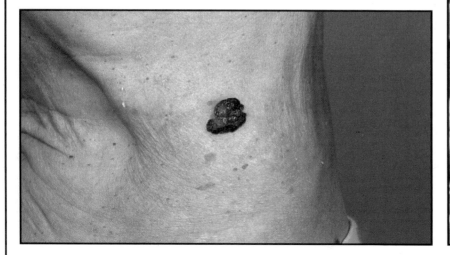

► When the amount of UV-B radiation reaching the earth's surface increases, the effects are particularly severe in urban areas.

In cities with heavily congested traffic, the levels of nitrogen oxides from car exhaust fumes are high. These substances react with sunlight to form harmful photochemical smog (see page 10). Driving restrictions have been introduced in Mexico City, in order to reduce vehicle exhaust emissions from the city's 3 million vehicles. The sign (inset) informs drivers of a traffic ban.

Dos and don'ts in the sunshine
DO
* Wear protective clothing and a hat with a wide brim
* Use a sunscreen with a high sun protection factor (SPF)
* Wear good-quality sunglasses that block out the UV radiation

DON'T
* Stay outdoors for long, without protective clothing, between 10 a.m. and 3 p.m.
* Allow your skin to become sunburned

AN OZONE HISTORY

In 1992, according to the NASA space agency the ozone layer over much of the Northern Hemisphere, including parts of North America, Russia, and northern Europe, was depleted by up to 40 percent. Here, we look back at certain developments that have led to the ozone crisis.

1920s The first aerosol spray cans were used in Norway.

1950 Commercial production of first CFC-containing aerosol hairspray cans.

1970 Scientists express concern about danger to the ozone layer from supersonic aircraft.

1974 US annual production of aerosol sprays reaches 3 billion.

1978 American government bans manufacture of CFCs for aerosol propellants. NASA launches Nimbus 7 weather satellite to monitor stratospheric ozone.

1984 British scientist Joe Farman confirms the existence of an "ozone hole" over the Antarctic.

1985 Annual worldwide production of CFCs reaches 700,000 tons.

1989 Levels of chlorine monoxide over the Arctic are 50 times higher than expected.

1957
International Geophysical Year. The British Antarctic Survey begins monitoring ozone levels at Halley Bay in Antarctica.

1940s
World War II troops use mosquito repellant in CFC-containing aerosols.

1928
Atoms of fluorine combine with carbon and chlorine to form CFCs. They were discovered by an American scientist, Thomas Midgely.

1974
American scientists warn of the link between CFCs and ozone depletion.

▲ **The Total Ozone Mapping Spectrometer (above) is used to monitor ozone levels from the Nimbus 7 weather satellite. It measures ozone from ground level up to the stratosphere.**

Monitoring ozone levels

In 1990, scientists from France, Germany, and the United States monitored ozone levels over the Arctic. They launched a series of balloons (see below), carrying measuring instruments and other experimental equipment. Some balloons flew as high as 17 miles above the earth.

The 1992 European Arctic Stratospheric Ozone Experiment monitored the extent of ozone depletion using similar equipment.

The Nimbus 7 weather satellite (left), which was first launched in 1978, carried eight different instruments to monitor the environment.

NASA headquarters (below)

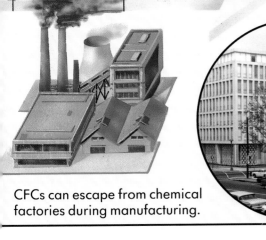

CFCs can escape from chemical factories during manufacturing.

OZONE FRIENDLY

Human beings have already pumped enough CFCs into the atmosphere to attack the ozone layer for decades. In 1990, aerosols still accounted for around 15 percent of CFC-12 sales.

To prevent further damage to this fragile shield, scientists from the World Resources Institute in the United States have drawn up a four-point plan to control CFC output: (1) reduce leakages, (2) encourage CFC collection and recycling, (3) replace the more harmful CFCs with less damaging or "soft" CFCs, and (4) develop manufacturing processes and products that do not use CFCs.

Chemicals called hydrocarbons and hydrochlorofluorocarbons (HCFCs) are now used to manufacture many kinds of foam containers, and also as aerosol propellants. However, both these alternatives contribute to the greenhouse effect, and HCFCs also release chlorine into the atmosphere.

The alternatives

Although the manufacture of CFCs for use in aerosols was banned in the United States in 1978, during the 1980s, world levels of CFCs continued to rise. They were increasingly used in aerosols manufactured in other countries, and in other products made in the United States. Today, an estimated 4,000 million spray cans are sold in the United States each year.

Many aerosol manufacturers in the developed world have now replaced CFCs with other "ozone-friendly" propellant gases (see right). Others are replacing CFC-containing aerosols with pump-action spray containers (shown far right), which do not need a propellant gas. Two large American producers of CFCs, Du Pont and Allied Signal, are now spending billions of dollars in developing replacement chemicals to CFCs.

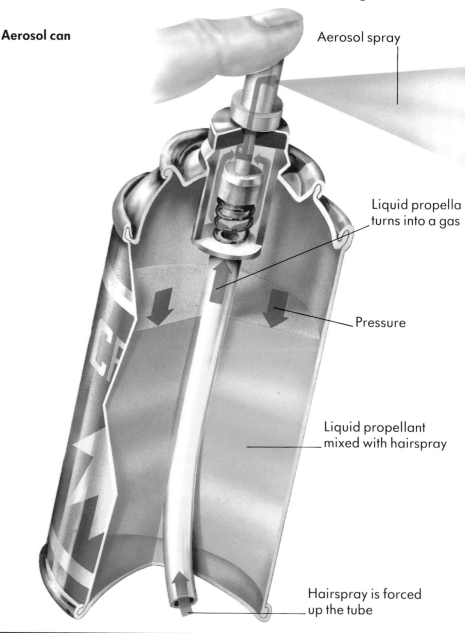

Aerosol can

Aerosol spray

Liquid propellant turns into a gas

Pressure

Liquid propellant mixed with hairspray

Hairspray is forced up the tube

► In Portsmouth, England, the local council operates a free gas reclamation service. It removes the CFCs from unwanted refrigerators and freezers (shown right), cleans the gas and then sells it back to industry.

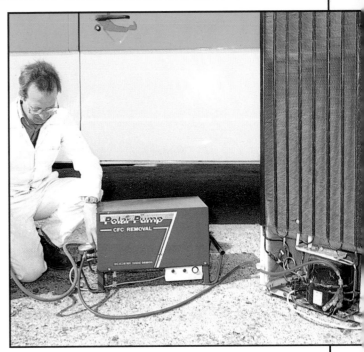

▲ The chemical industry is developing CFC-free products for use in processes such as foam blowing. In the fast food industry, some CFC-blown boxes and cartons are being replaced with more ozone-friendly packaging (above).

The soft option

So-called "soft" CFCs have replaced the more dangerous CFC-11 and CFC-12 in some appliances. However, even these will deplete ozone levels by adding small amounts of chlorine to the atmosphere. Some manufacturers now use a mixture of propane and butane to produce "CFC-free" refrigerators, while ammonia can replace CFCs in large-scale refrigeration units.

WHAT CAN WE DO?

The most important task in the fight to protect the ozone layer is to control emissions of CFCs. The 1987 Montreal Protocol on Substances that Deplete the Ozone Layer called for consumption of the five main CFCs to drop by 50 percent by 1999.

Continuing concern about the ever-increasing ozone loss led to the 1990 Saving the Ozone Layer conference in London, which agreed to phase out completely the production and consumption of all CFCs and halons in developed countries by the year 2000. In November 1992, the phase-out date for CFCs was brought forward to 1995. Developing countries are allowed a further 10 years in which to phase out the banned substances.

To assist the development of CFC-free chemicals and technology in the developing world, a special fund of $240 million was set up in 1990.

▼ **The Upper Atmosphere Research Satellite was launched during a mission of the US space shuttle Discovery in September 1991. In 1992, the satellite sent back information showing that the levels of harmful chlorine monoxide over parts of the northern hemisphere were the highest ever.**

▶ People in countries like China and India have only recently been able to buy domestic appliances such as refrigerators. China produces 8 million refrigeratiors each year, and the percentage of refrigerator-owning households has risen dramatically. In 1991, the Chinese government announced that it had ratified the Montreal Protocol.

◀ In May 1989, a total of 80 countries attended the first meeting of the parties to the Montreal Protocol in Finland. The meeting decided to eliminate the production of CFCs by the year 2000.

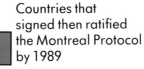

Countries that signed then ratified the Montreal Protocol by 1989

Countries that signed the Montreal Protocol by 1991

By the middle of 1991, 70 countries had signed the Montreal Protocol. However, there is some evidence that chemicals like halons, which are now banned in much of the developed world, are being sold to countries that have not yet signed the Protocol.

THE FUTURE

According to the World Meteorological Organization, ozone levels in both hemispheres have dropped by an average of three percent in the past 10 years. Some studies point to ozone depletion of between four and eight percent in the Northern Hemisphere.

There have been some successes in the fight to protect the earth's ozone layer. In February 1992, the United States and EC countries banned the use and production of most CFCs by the end of 1995, some 5 years ahead of the date agreed under the Montreal Protocol. In November 1992, the Protocol's timetable for banning CFCs was also altered to 1995. Sixteen of the world's leading chemical companies have joined forces to speed up the development of alternative chemicals to CFCs.

However, throughout the world, governments must continue the fight against CFCs and other ozone-depleting chemicals. The current levels of CFC use mean that the amount of chlorine in the atmosphere will continue to increase, at least until 1997.

◀ The 1992 Earth Summit in Rio de Janeiro, Brazil, discussed ways of tackling the world's environmental problems. Despite recent measures to control the output of CFCs, scientists estimate that ozone levels will fall by a further 15 percent by the year 2000.

In November 1992, the UN sponsored the ozone layer conference in Denmark. Representatives from over 90 countries agreed to extend the Montreal Protocol to cover HCFCs and methyl bromide for the first time.

The production of HCFCs will be limited from 1996, with a total ban by 2030. Methyl bromide production will be frozen at 1991 levels by 1995, but will not be phased out until several years later. Environmentalists claim that these new controls are not strict enough.

▶ At the 1992 Global Forum in Brazil, representatives of indigenous peoples (shown right) and non-governmental organizations met to discuss environmental issues.

Many developing countries argue that the industrialized nations should accept responsibility for creating the ozone hole, and should finance solutions to the problem.

The 1992 Conference discussed the possibility of providing additional finance to help developing countries to comply with the revised Montreal Protocol.

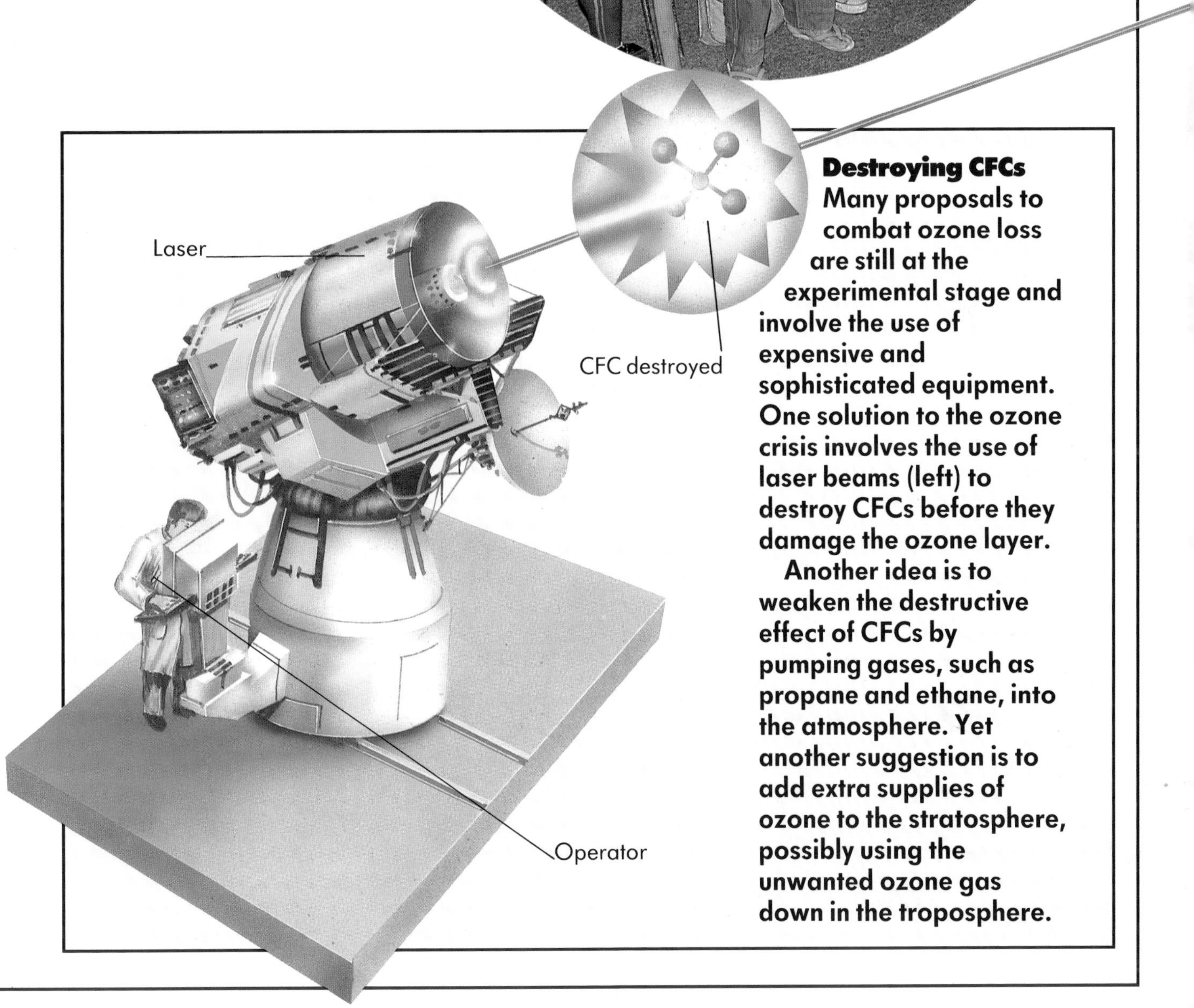

Laser

CFC destroyed

Operator

Destroying CFCs

Many proposals to combat ozone loss are still at the experimental stage and involve the use of expensive and sophisticated equipment. One solution to the ozone crisis involves the use of laser beams (left) to destroy CFCs before they damage the ozone layer.

Another idea is to weaken the destructive effect of CFCs by pumping gases, such as propane and ethane, into the atmosphere. Yet another suggestion is to add extra supplies of ozone to the stratosphere, possibly using the unwanted ozone gas down in the troposphere.

FACT FILE

Use of CFCs

To date, 95 percent of the damage to the ozone layer is due to the release of CFCs from the West. The United States produces 30 percent of the world's CFCs, while the European Community accounts for between 40 and 50 percent of global CFC production. The developing world is responsible for no more than 16 percent of world CFC consumption.

Global warming

If the production of greenhouse gases continues to rise at its present rate, scientists predict that the earth's surface temperature will increase by about 1° F during each decade in the next 100 years. This global warming could result in sea levels around the world rising by as much as 8 in by the year 2030.

Freon

Freon is the trade name given to CFCs manufactured by the Dupont company, the world's largest CFC producer. CFC-12 (Freon-12) is principally used as a coolant in refrigeration units. Production of Freon increased by a staggering 4,000 percent between 1931 and 1945.

In the United States, many car service centers are installing machinery to recycle the CFC-12 that is used in automobile air-conditioning units.

Ozone over Britain

Joe Farman, the British scientist who confirmed the existence of the Antarctic ozone hole, claims that a 20 percent ozone loss during the spring months might occur over Britain by the year 2000.

Methyl bromide

Methyl bromide may be responsible for up to 10 percent of current ozone depletion. This toxic gas gives off bromine, which is between 30 and 60 times more effective than chlorine at destroying ozone. Its main use is to sterilize soil so that crops like strawberries can be grown all year round. Methyl bromide is also used to fumigate ships and aircraft holds, as well as foods such as grapes, wheat, rice, and coffee.

Controls on CFCs

1972 – United Nations Environment Program (UNEP) created following a UN conference on the human environment. UNEP promotes environmental awareness and encourages cooperation between governments on environmental issues.
1985 – intergovernmental discussions organized by UNEP result in 20 countries signing the Vienna Convention on the Protection of the Ozone Layer.
1987 – Montreal Protocol on Substances that Deplete the Ozone Layer agrees to cut CFC production to 1986 levels by 1989, leading to a 50 percent reduction in consumption by 1999.
1989 – Helsinki conference agrees to worldwide ban on CFCs by the year 2000.
1990 – London conference of countries that signed the Montreal Protocol. Time-table decided for ending CFC production and use.
1992 – United Nations Conference on the Environment and Development (UNCED) in Rio de Janeiro – the Earth Summit. Convention on climate change signed by more than 150 countries.

Meeting in Denmark of the parties to the Montreal Protocol.

Ozone at ground level

Ozone pollution is made worse when the air temperature rises. The Environmental Protection Agency (EPA) has estimated that a temperature increase of 6° F in a densely populated area, such as San Francisco Bay, could lead to a 20 percent increase in the amount of ozone contained in the air.

A continuing problem

We have already added 320 million or so tons of CFC into the atmosphere. They are likely to remain there for all of this century and much of the next one. Scientists expect damage to the ozone layer to continue until at least the year 2000.

GLOSSARY

aerosol – a fine mist of tiny liquid droplets.

aerosol spray can – a container filled with a liquid, which is released in a fine spray. Often called "aerosol" for short.

atmosphere – the mixture of different gases that surround the earth.

atom – the smallest part of all gases, liquids, and solid materials.

bromine – a gas that is released into the atmosphere by halons and by methyl bromide. It destroys ozone.

cancer – a disease that damages or destroys healthy parts of the human body.

cataract – clouding of the lens of the eye, which causes poor eyesight.

chlorine – a gas that is released into the atmosphere by CFCs and destroys ozone.

chlorofluorocarbons (CFCs) – a group of man-made chemicals used to manufacture aerosols, refrigerators, and some plastics.

deplete – to reduce.

food chain – a group of living things that are linked together because each living thing eats the one before it in the chain, and is then eaten by the one after it.

global warming – the gradual heating-up of the earth as a result of too much heat being trapped inside the earth's atmosphere.

greenhouse effect – the trapping of heat from the sun's rays by gases in the atmosphere. The heat helps to keep the earth warm.

greenhouse gas – one of the gases in the atmosphere that traps the heat from the sun's rays so that it cannot escape into space.

halon – a gas that is used inside fire extinguishers.

molecule – a small part of a substance that is made up from one or more atoms.

ozone – a pale blue gas with a very strong smell. It is a form of oxygen.

ozone hole – the disappearance of half or more of the ozone layer that surrounds the earth from a specific area.

ozone layer – a band of ozone gas that is found in the upper atmosphere. It protects the earth from the sun's harmful rays.

photochemical smog – a kind of air pollution that is formed at ground level. It contains ozone.

photosynthesis – the process of a green plant using the energy from sunlight to change water and carbon dioxide into the carbohydrates it needs to grow.

plankton – tiny plants and animals that live on and just below the surface of the sea. Plankton are at the bottom of all marine food chains.

pollutant – a waste substance that causes damage to the environment.

propellant – a substance that is used to help spray a liquid out of an aerosol spray can.

solvent – any liquid that dissolves or weakens a solid material.

stratosphere – a layer of the atmosphere that includes the protective ozone layer.

troposphere – the lowest layer of the atmosphere, which contains the air we breathe.

ultraviolet (UV) radiation – invisible rays from the sun, which cause skin to tan.

INDEX

Photographic credits:
Cover and pages 18, 19 both, 21 top & bottom, 27 & 28: Frank Spooner Pictures; title page & 7 both, 9, 12, 17, 20, 22 both & 23 top & middle: Science Photo Library; 8 & 23 bottom: NASA; 11 & 20-21: Eye Ubiquitous; 15 left & 29: Panos Pictures; 15 right & 25 top left & bottom: Roger Vlitos; 25 top right: Portsmouth City Council; 26: Spectrum Colour Library.